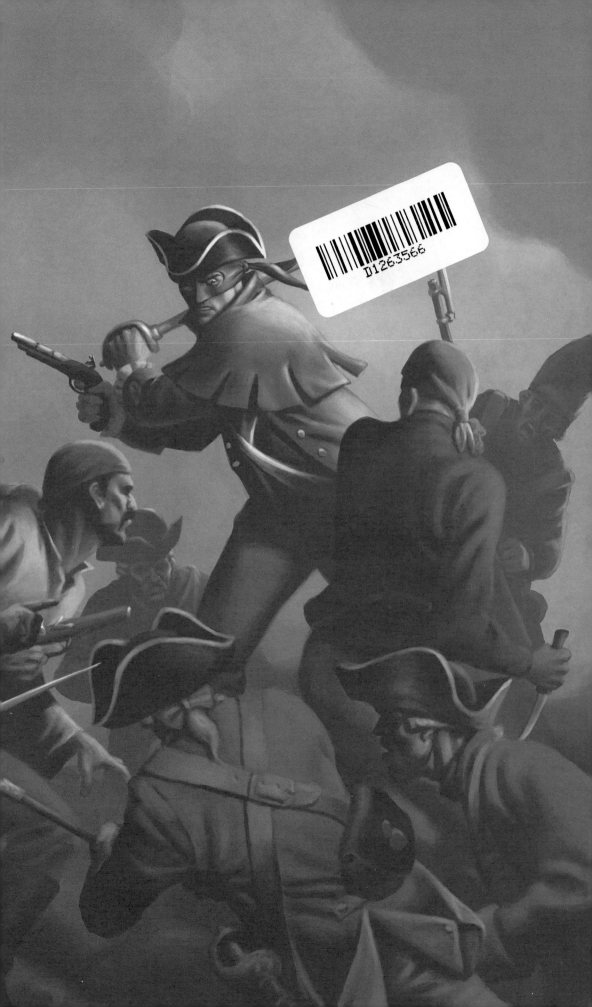

APE ENTERTAINMENT PRESENTS:

the Black Coat
A Call to Arms

Chapter 1
Written by:
BEN LICHIUS and
ADAM COGAN
Illustrated by:
FRANCESCO
FRANCAVILLA
Inked by:
JEREMY COLWELL
(pgs 1-9)
Lettered by:
CHRIS STUDABAKER
Editor:
BEN LICHIUS

Front Cover:
FRANCESCO
FRANCAVILLA
AND
EUAN
MACTAVISH

Chapter 2
Written by:
ADAM COGAN
Illustrated by:
FRANCESCO
FRANCAVILLA
Lettered by:
CHRIS STUDABAKER
Editor:
BEN LICHIUS

Chapter 3
Written by:
ADAM COGAN
Illustrated by:
FRANCESCO
FRANCAVILLA
Lettered by:
CHRIS STUDABAKER
Editor:
BEN LICHIUS

Chapter
Written by
ADAM COGAN
Illustrated b
FRANCESCO
FRANCAVILL
Lettered by
CHRIS STUDABA
Editor:
BEN LICHIUS

The year is 1775...

War threatens to break out in the colonies at any time - it could be weeks or even days away
Nowhere is the tension higher than in New York City, the bustling headquarters for all o
Britain's activities in the colonies.
Acting on behalf of the Continental Congress, The Knights of Liberty, led by the mysterious
masked spy known as "The Black Coat", work in secret against British forces in an effort to
combat further injustices by the Crown. The newly-appointed commander of military forces Lt
Gen. Henry Savidge is aware of The Black Coat's activities, but has so far been unable to stop
him. Out of desperation, Savidge has cut a deal with an ancient secret society that may mark an
end to colonial resistance - or perhaps the colonies themselves...

Ape Entertainment:
DIR. of FINANCE DAVID HEDGECOCK
DIR. of MARKETING BRENT E. ERWIN

Created by:
BEN LICHIUS and
FRANCESCO FRANCAVILLA

GUNPOWDER
PRESS

www.THE-BLACK-COAT.com
www.ApeComics.com

Chapter 1

MARCH, 1775

ONE MILE FROM NEW YORK CITY HARBOR.

This smells like a trap...

...

...and dead rats.

My men can't wait forever.

ZWMMWIPP

I have to put this ship out of commission as quickly as possible...

UNNGH.

...rats or no rats.

AHHH...

BONES, WOULD YOU BE SO KIND AS TO UNCOVER YOUR LANTERN SO'S I CAN SEE ME WATCH?

Damn.

Which one was it?

MR. BLACK COAT. LAST TIME WE MET WAS NONE TOO *PLEASANT* FOR ME, I MUST ADMIT.

SHE WAS *STURDY*, TOO. THE *SHRAPNEL* NEARLY TOOK ME HEAD OFF.

THE DEVIL'S HAND WAS A MIGHTY SHIP. SHE HAD AN ILLUSTRIOUS CAREER BEFORE YOU BLEW HER SKY HIGH.

BUT ENOUGH ABOUT THE PAST. I KNOW YOU'RE HERE SO'S YOU CAN STOP US FROM ATTACKIN' THE *SEADOVE* TOMORROW.

WHAT WITH IT CARRYIN' THE HONORABLE *COLONIAL AMBASSADOR* AND ALL.

SO'S I WANT YA TO KNOW ONE THING BEFORE WE KILL YA'...

...'TIS NOTHIN' PERSONAL, LAD. ONLY MONEY.

TRUTH BE TOLD, EVEN WITH ALL WE BEEN THROUGH, I'M KINDA SAD TO SEE YA GO.

I LIKE YOUR STYLE.

I'M GLAD TO HEAR THAT YOU DON'T HOLD ANY GRUDGES, BLITHE...

...I ALWAYS SAY, IT'S NEVER TOO LATE TO SHAKE HANDS AND BE FRIENDS.

KA-CHIK

THAT'S MIGHTY KIND, BUT I'M AFRAID WE'RE STILL GONNA KILL YA'.

DON'T TAKE IT *TOO* HARD, LAD.

NO WORRIES, BLITHE. I ALWAYS KNEW I WOULD GO OUT WITH A BANG.

BANG

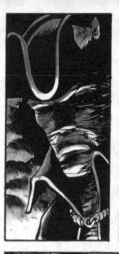

have tonight are out of our hands.

EVENIN' SIR.

SEE ANYTHING YOU LIKE?

YOU HAVE NICE...ARMS.

A FEW HOURS LATER...

AMBASSADOR! WELCOME HOME. SAFE AND SOUND, I SEE.

HONESTLY, NATHANIEL, I DON'T SEE WHY YOU WORRY OVER ME LIKE A MOTHER HEN EVERY TIME I LEAVE THE NEST.

A LITTLE *QUEASINESS* ASIDE, THE VOYAGE WAS UTTERLY WITHOUT *INCIDENT*.

YESSIR.

THOMAS, GRAB MR. FRANKLIN'S LUGGAGE, WOULD YOU?

SO, HOW WAS ENGLAND, BEN?

NINE WASTED YEARS. DID YOU HEAR HOW THEY HUMILIATED ME IN PARLIAMENT?

THEY STILL THINK WE COLONISTS ARE THEIR ERRANT CHILDREN. BUT IT ONLY SERVED TO STRENGTHEN MY RESOLVE.

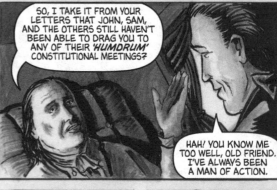

SO, I TAKE IT FROM YOUR LETTERS THAT JOHN, SAM, AND THE OTHERS STILL HAVEN'T BEEN ABLE TO DRAG YOU TO ANY OF THEIR *'HUMDRUM'* CONSTITUTIONAL MEETINGS?

HAH! YOU KNOW ME TOO WELL, OLD FRIEND. I'VE ALWAYS BEEN A MAN OF ACTION.

I NEVER UNDERSTOOD HOW THEY COULD ACCOMPLISH ANYTHING WITH ALL THAT *POSTURING* AND *POSTULATING*.

I'M SURE THINGS WILL CHANGE NOW THAT WE HAVE THE BENEFIT OF YOUR WISDOM.

KER-
CRASH

BATES
ROYAL FUNERAL
SERVICES

THAT NIGHT.

I BELIEVE THAT WE'RE ALL AT THE MERCY OF OUR FATHER IN HEAVEN, BUT I DON'T BELIEVE THAT HE MAKES A HABIT OF REMOVING A PERSON'S ARMS AND THEN DISCARDING THE BODY IN THE HUDSON.

BUT TO BE SURE, THIS IS A CASE OF FOUL PLAY IS IT NOT, MR. BATES?

THE CAUSE OF DEATH IS NOT CLEAR.

IT IS POSSIBLE THAT THE WOMAN DIED BY NATURAL MEANS AND THEN, UPON FINDING HER, SOME UNSAVORY CRIMINAL TOOK THE OPPORTUNITY TO PERFORM THESE HEINOUS ACTS.

FOR WHAT PURPOSE, HOWEVER, I-I CAN NOT FATHOM.

INDIANS?

I SUPPOSE IT IS POSSIBLE.

SAVAGES.

BUT LOOK AT THE WOUNDS. HARDLY CHARACTERISTIC OF NATIVE WEAPONS.

NO, I BELIEVE THIS UNFORTUNATE GIRL FELL PREY TO A MORE SOPHISTICATED BEAST.

"UNFORTUNATE?"

SHE WAS A COMMON HARLOT. THE ONLY ONES WHO'LL MISS HER COMPANY ARE ADULTEROUS DRUNKARDS AND SAILORS ON SHORE LEAVE.

WELL, I MUST BE ON MY WAY.

IT IS GETTING LATE AND I HAVE TO MAKE A REPORT TO LT-GENERAL SAVIDGE.

COME THEN. I WILL SEE YOU TO THE DOOR.

Would that we could have one murder in this town that our dear constable did not try to blame on the natives...

Josephine Townsend...

How I hoped my suspicions were wrong.

It was Townsend who tipped me off about Captain Blithe and the Graveyard...

...but why assassinate her?

Was she found out? Or was she in fact a traitor, dicarded when she was no longer useful?

I hate this. I can't even mourn her properly for fear she may have betrayed me.

No. This is a young woman lying before me.

She was the first of my agents to die in my service. and she was a good friend.

She deserves to be mourned.

And someone deserves to pay for her murder.

These incisions were made by someone with a knowledge of anatomy.

But what could the enemy possibly want with her limbs?

Ah, her locket.

I'm sure Robin will want it.

ACROSS TOWN.

THIS LETTER JUST ARRIVED, GOV.

AH. I WAS WONDERING WHEN WE'D BE SUMMONED.

I'M SURE MY DEAR BROTHER WON'T MIND IF I OPEN IT.

Wilhelm Krauss

WILL THAT BE ALL, GOV?

THERE IS *ONE* MORE THING, OTTO...

BE SURE TO KILL THAT CLUMSY *DUMMKOPF* YOU WORK WITH FOR ME, WOULD YOU?

SURE THING, GOV.

WOULDN'T WANT TO BE GETTIN' RUSTY, NOW WOULD I?

Josephine Townsend was new and *inexperienced.* Easy prey for the *monster* that killed her.

My guess is he'll strike again. And I'll be ready for him.

Townsend's death is evidence enough that she was *not* working for the British.

She was likely an unwitting victim. *Purposefully* fed information in order to set a *trap* for me.

Lt-General Savidge would *certainly* have used her against me if presented with the opportunity.

But to have her...*butchered* for being a spy against the Crown?

No, I doubt he could give such an order. His gentlemanly pride would not allow it.

I sense another hand at work--

I SEE THAT YOU GOT MY MESSAGE.

ACROSS TOWN, AT BRITISH MILITARY HEADQUARTERS.

--THE ONLY ONES WHO'LL MISS HER ARE *ADULTEROUS* DRUNKARDS AND *SAILORS* ON SHORE LEAVE.

IT'S AN ODD CASE, BUT I FEEL IT'S NOTHING TO CONCERN OURSELVES WITH, GENERAL.

VERY GOOD, CONSTABLE. I HAVE YOUR REPORT.

YOU SHOULD GET SOME REST. YOU'LL NEED IT IF THESE *SAVAGES* ARE STILL ON THE LOOSE.

I TRUST YOU'LL SEE YOURSELF OUT?

YES, SIR. THANK YOU, SIR.

IS THIS HOW YOUR MEN WORK? *SLAUGHTERING* HELPLESS WOMEN AND *DUMPING* THEM IN THE RIVER?

YOU'RE SUPPOSED TO HELP ME *TAKE CONTROL* OF THIS CITY, NOT THROW IT INTO A *PANIC*.

PATIENCE, LIEUTENANT-GENERAL.

SOMETIMES... THERE IS A METHOD TO OUR MADNESS.

MY MEN WILL GIVE YOU THE RESULTS YOU WANT.

UNLIKE THE PETTY MACHINATIONS OF YOUR IDIOT KING, *THE LEAGUE* KNOWS THAT THE KEY TO THIS CITY...

...AND TO THE COLONIES...

...LIES WITH ONE MAN...

...THE BLACK COAT.

Chapter 2

❧ NEW YORK CITY - MARCH 14, 1775 ❧

LIBERTY IS OUR GUIDING LIGHT.

IN DARKNESS WE WAGE THE FIGHT.

HERE LIES JOSEPHINE TOWNSEND, MY DEAR FRIEND.

I WANTED TO THANK YOU FOR RETRIEVING JOSEPHINE'S LOCKET.

I...HAVEN'T YET SUMMONED THE STRENGTH TO PASS IT ON TO HER DAUGHTER.

ROBIN'S A SWEET GIRL. LET'S GIVE HER A FEW MORE DAYS OF PEACE.

THEY STUCK ME IN THAT MOLDERING TOMB...

...LEFT ME FOR THE WORMS TO FIND. BUT MY RESOURCEFUL BROTHER FOUND ME FIRST.

'SNIP'

AND THEY *WOULD* HAVE, IF I LET THEM *CATCH* ME.

I THOUGHT WE HAD LEFT SUCH MANIA BEHIND US. YOU TAKE FOOLISH RISKS LATELY, AND FOR WHAT REASONS I CANNOT FATHOM.

SHOULD HAVE BURIED YOU BESIDE ME, EH?

YOU HAVE EVERYTHING YOU NEED HERE. WHY MUST YOU KEEP GOING OUT?

THAT IS MY CONCERN!

NO, WILHELM! NOT *THIS* TIME! I DON'T WANT TO BE BURIED BESIDE YOU. NOT HERE IN THIS FESTERING COLONY. NOT FOR SOME FOOL OBSESSION.

YOU WON'T BE SATISFIED UNTIL THAT COSTUMED PHANTOM TAKES YOUR CONFOUNDED *HEAD* ALONG WITH YOUR ARM.

HE CAN ONLY *KILL* ME, AND THAT IS AN EMPTY THREAT NOW. IF YOU MUST WORRY, WORRY ABOUT *THE LEAGUE*.

THEIR PUNISHMENTS ARE...*SEVERE*.

The Butcher chose sailors instead of strumpets tonight. Why?

These surgical striations. He must be using a new tool of some kind.

I wonder where someone might acquire such an instrument?

LOOK 'ERE BOYS...

LOOKS LIKE WE CAUGHT OUR BUTCHER IN THE ACT!

AYE, AND WE GOT HIM SNUG AS A CORK IN A BOTTLE OF CLARET.

WE GAVE CHASE AND BARRED THE ROADS, BUT HE SLIPPED PAST OUR CHECK POINTS JUST THE SAME. IT'S PASSING STRANGE, SIR.

AND THERE WERE CIVILIAN WITNESSES?

OH, YES SIR. HALF THE CITY TURNED OUT FOR THE FIREWORKS. MOST OF THE LOT KNEW WHO WE WERE AFTER-- AND WHAT HE DID.

THANK YOU, SERGEANT. YOU'RE DISMISSED. CLOSE THE DOOR BEHIND YOU.

--HOPPED FROM ROOF TO ROOF LIKE A MONKEY.

YOU HEARD?

A RIDICULOUS NOTION, OF COURSE. WE BOTH KNOW IT WAS *YOUR* MAN WHO COMMITTED THIS NEW ATROCITY.

I MUST ONCE AGAIN IMPLORE YOU TO PUT A STOP TO THIS BUTCHER BEFORE--

--I AM ALREADY WEARY OF THIS ARGUMENT.

DO YOU NOT SEE THE OPPORTUNITY PRESENTED BEFORE US?

I THINK SO, YES.

A COURT MARSHAL FOLLOWED BY A MERCIFUL HANGING.

STARVE A FIRE AND IT DIES.

FEED IT, AND IT GROWS AND SPREADS LIKE A LIVING THING.

WE WILL FEED THIS FIRE, GENERAL.

AND... *SNIFF*...

IT'S ALRIGHT, ROBIN. TAKE YOUR TIME.

...TORIES ALL OVER TOWN CRY OUT FOR JUSTICE--THEY BLAME THE BLACK COAT FOR THE BUTCHER'S *DEVILRY*!

YOU'VE DONE WELL, ROBIN. THANK YOU FOR BRINGING THIS TO OUR ATTENTION.

YOU HEARD HER, KNIGHTS--THESE ARE GRIM TIDINGS, AND NO MISTAKE.

IT'S AN EASY FALL FROM ONE'S GOOD STANDING, AND A HARD CLIMB BACK UP.

BUT WHAT WILL WE DO?

WE MUST CONVINCE THE MAN OF THE HOUR TO BE A LITTLE MORE DISCREET, MY DEAR.

MEANWHILE THE REST OF US WILL VENTURE INTO THE CITY AND SPREAD THE TRUTH ABOUT OUR LEADER--

--WHEREVER THE NEED IS GREATEST AND THE RED COATS ARE SCARCEST.

TELL THEM *THE BLACK COAT* IS A MAN ABOVE REPROACH! HE, MORE THAN ANYONE, HAS DEVOTED HIMSELF FULLY TO PROTECTING THE COLONY AND ALL HER PEOPLE.

RAMSEY TR

NOW GO FORTH!

CHRISTOPHER, SILAS, LYMAN-- STAY A MOMENT. WE HAVE MORE TO DISCUSS.

IN MY OFFICE, PLEASE.

RAMSE

YOU WILL RECALL CAPTAIN BLITHE, LATELY OF THE GRAVEYARD?

AYE, BEFORE THE BLACK COAT GAVE IT A BURIAL AT SEA.

ALL THREE OF YOU PLAYED A ROLE THAT NIGHT. BUT LISTEN CLOSE--THIS CONCERNS THE ENTIRE ORGANIZATION.

KNOW THIS--A SECRET GROUP NOW WORKS TO UNDERMINE ALL OUR ENDEAVORS. OUR INTELLIGENCE IS WOEFULLY INCOMPLETE. WE'VE BUT SPOTTED HER MASTS TOPPING THE WAVE.

IT WAS THIS NEW ENEMY, NOT THE BRITISH, WHO HIRED CAPTAIN BLITHE AND HIS CREW TO KILL BEN FRANKLIN THAT NIGHT YOU THREE WERE ABOARD THE SCYLLA.

I BELIEVE JOSEPHINE TOWNSEND GOT WIND OF THEIR PLAN SOMEHOW, AND THAT THE BUTCHER MURDERED HER ON THEIR BEHALF.

SHE WAS ONE OF US. SHE DESERVED BETTER.

BLITHE HAD AN OLD STRONGHOLD ON ROATAN ISLAND, OFF THE COAST OF JAMAICA. THAT IS OUR BEST LEAD.

SAY HELLO TO BARNABAS STARKEY. HE SAILED 'ROUND THE EAST INDIES WITH ME BACK IN THE OLD DAYS WHEN THE RAMSEY TRADE COMPANY DID MORE PRIVATEERING THAN TRADING.

HOW TIMES DO CHANGE, M'LADY.

WHAT'S ALL THIS TO DO WITH YOU THREE?

AS IT HAPPENS, BARNABAS IS A MAN SHORT. SINCE YOU THREE ARE VETERAN SAILORS, I NEED A VOLUNTEER TO SAIL WITH HIM TO JAMAICA AND HELP HIM CRACK SOME PIRATE SKULLS.

BARNABAS WORKS WITH THE CARIBBEAN CHAPTER OF THE KNIGHTS OF LIBERTY THESE DAYS. HE HAS AGREED TO DEPART FORTHWITH AND SNIFF OUT THE TRAIL OF THE UNFORTUNATE CAPTAIN BLITHE.

ER...I...
I WILL, URSULA. I'VE NOT BEEN SO FAR SOUTH, BUT I'LL HELP AS I MAY.

WELL DONE, LYMAN. YOU ARE A CREDIT TO THE KNIGHTS OF LIBERTY.

RIGHT, THEN, OFF YOU GO, BOYS.

REMEMBER—BE VIGILANT. KEEP AN EAR TO THE GROUND AND AN EYE TO THE SHADOWS.

THANKS FOR COMING ON SUCH SHORT NOTICE, MY FRIEND. IT'S GOOD TO SEE YOU.

AND YOU, LOVE.

GET A GOOD LOOK?

AYE, I'D KNOW 'EM IF THEY WAS TARRED, FEATHERED, AND DRESSED AS INDIANS.

GOOD. HAVE A FEW OF YOUR MEN STAY BEHIND AND SHADOW CHRIS CLEMEN AND SILAS HOBB. WE NEED OUTSIDERS ON THIS.

THEY WERE THE ONLY AGENTS WHO KNEW OF OUR PLANS TO ATTACK THE GRAVEYARD.

SINCE LYMAN WAS WILLING TO LEAVE, I'M CERTAIN WE CAN ELIMINATE HIM FROM SUSPICION.

I AM CONVINCED THAT JOSEPHINE TOWNSEND WAS INNOCENT OF TREASON. THAT MEANS...

...ONE OF THOSE TWO IS SURELY AN ENEMY SPY!

Oliver Vines is a master craftsman. His Foundry is the largest and the finest in America.

The surgeons of Belle Vue come to him whenever they need something special.

If the Butcher commissioned Vines to forge some murderous tool, then surely Vines kept some records.

Vines?

THE BLACK COAT.

SUCH A CLEVER MAN.

I KNEW YOU WOULD COME.

Chapter 3

...TURNING THE PEOPLE AGAINST *THE BLACK COAT* AND *BLAMING* HIM FOR YOUR MAN'S MURDER STREAK WAS A STROKE OF BLOODY *GENIUS.*

I REALLY MUST HAND IT TO YOU, LORD MORROW...

LOOK AT ME, SAVIDGE.

DO YOU SEE A MAN WHO IS PRONE TO *FLATTERY?*

BESIDES, YOUR OPTIMISM IS PREMATURE. THE BLACK COAT REMAINS *FREE.*

A TRIFLING FORMALITY. HIS OWN *SUPPORTERS* WILL BRING HIM DOWN-- IT'S JUST A MATTER OF TIME.

IN ANY CASE, I BELIEVE YOUR BUSINESS IN NEW YORK HAS CONCLUDED, AND YOU'LL BE RETURNING TO ENGLAND?

NO.

THE LEAGUE HAS ASSIGNED ME TO THIS COMMAND FOR THE DURATION OF THE WAR.

WAR?!!?

FORGIVE ME, SAVIDGE. NOW *I'M* BEING *PREMATURE.*

KNOCK-KNOCK

YES?

PARDON THE INTRUSION, SIR--

I...I THOUGHT... DO YOU HAVE COMPANY, SIR?

WHAT IS IT YOU WANT, SERGEANT?

MISTER KRAUSS HAS ARRIVED, SIR.

SHOW HIM IN.

BE SEATED, FREDRICK.

YOU HAVE GOOD NEWS, I TRUST.

MY BROTHER HAS MADE PROGRESS, YES--THANKS TO THE GENEROUS FACILITIES THE LEAGUE HAS PROVIDED.

THE LEAGUE HAS INVESTED MUCH IN YOUR BROTHER'S RESEARCH.

WE EXPECT NOTHING LESS THAN TOTAL SUCCESS.

INITIAL TESTS ARE MODESTLY FAVORABLE. HE BELIEVES HE WILL COMPLETE THE FORMULA IN A MATTER OF DAYS.

HOWEVER, HE HAS BEEN IMPEDED BY THIS MEDDLING MASKED MARAUDER OF YOURS.

IMPEDED? FROM SLAYING STRUMPETS, YOU MEAN?

YOU NEED NOT CONCERN YOURSELF, MISTER KRAUSS.

ONE OF OUR AGENTS HAS PENETRATED THE BLACK COAT'S ORGANIZATION. WE ARE NOW PRIVY TO EVERY PLOT AND SCHEME AGAINST YOUR BROTHER.

NEXT TIME, WE WILL ACT UPON THAT FOREKNOWLEDGE.

"Well, I was already running late, so I hit upon the idea of cutting through Fly Market."

"Normally I steer clear of the place."

"It's always full of *unsavories*."

"Well, one of them sailors latched onto me like a lamprey."

"I knew he'd keep after me..."

"...so I steeled myself for a confrontation on my terms."

"But the moment never came."

"THE BUTCHER."

--LIKE THAT FELLOW IN MOLDAVIA LAST YEAR, OR THOSE TROUBLES WITH THE PENOBSCOT INDIANS...

YES, *HIM.* I ASSUME HE'S ANOTHER ONE OF THESE "PECULIARITIES" YOU KEEP RUNNING INTO--

OH YES, HE'S PASSING PECULIAR.

I'VE INFLICTED WOUNDS THAT WOULD HAVE PROVEN *THOROUGHLY* FATAL TO AN ORDINARY MAN. HE SIMPLY REFUSES TO *DIE.*

I AM COMPLETELY AT A LOSS.

YOU WILL FIND THE ANSWER, MY FRIEND. YOU ALWAYS DO.

FIGHTING HIM AGAIN WOULD BE FOOLHARDY WITH *YOUR* INJURIES.

BUT YOU NEED NOT FIGHT HIM *ALONE,* YOU KNOW.

YOU HAVE SIXTY KNIGHTS OF LIBERTY READY TO AID YOU, IF YOU WOULD ONLY *LET* THEM.

"Well, there's one detail we all heard about."

"Her Father would turn in his grave if he knew she was squandering the Ramsey Fortune on all the dockside doxies in town."

"I dunno, Hobb. I suppose she wanted to get them off the street in order to limit the Butcher's choices..."

BARLOWE'S TAVERN

"...'till there was only one."

EVENING, SIR.

CARE TO BUY SOME FLOWERS FOR THE MISSUS?

I GO THROUGH ALL THE TROUBLE OF FETCHING *PHOBOS* FOR YOU, AND HERE YOU ARE WALKING.

WE'LL NEVER CATCH THEM AT THIS PACE. GET CAUGHT *OURSELVES*, MORE LIKE.

PATIENCE, BARNABAS. LOOK HERE.

WHAT IS IT YOU'RE UP TO?

URSULA LEFT A TRAIL.

TOO MANY IF YOU ASK ME.

LET'S HOPE SHE HAD ENOUGH FLOWERS.

DAMN.

UNNNGH...

W-WHERE...?

DEAR GOD...

Chapter 4

Studying the extract led me to my first groundbreaking discoveries.

My results were temporary and unstable, but I knew I could improve upon the formula.

And then...success!

When I announced my triumph at Oxford, they marveled at the science, they talked about what it would mean for surgeons and amputees--but they failed to see the larger ramifications.

I had vanquished *death itself*--all for you, Mary.

MARY IS *DEAD*, WILHELM. DO TRY TO REMEMBER. IT HAPPENED JUST AFTER THE EXHIBITION.

SHE DIED... AND THEN SHE BECAME A *HORROR.* YOU HAD TO KILL HER AGAIN IN THE END.

THIS ISN'T MARY. YOU SEE?

WHEN WAS THE LAST TIME YOU TOOK YOUR SERUM? YOU'RE STARTING TO SEE THINGS AGAIN, DEAR BROTHER.

MARY?

NEVER MIND. AS LONG AS SHE DOESN'T INTERFERE WITH YOUR WORK.

LORD MORROW SENT US ANOTHER INVITATION. THIS IS THE *LAST TIME* I WILL GO ON YOUR BEHALF TO EXPLAIN WHY THE SERUM IS NOT YET PERFECTED.

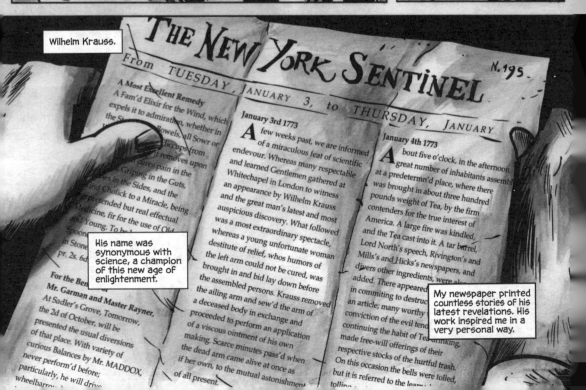

WE'RE RIGHT GLAD TO FIND YOU, YOUNG JACKANAPES! YOU WOUNDED?

JUST A FEW SCRATCHES.

URSULA...

I DON'T KNOW WHETHER TO KISS YOU OR--OR *SHAKE* YOU FOR CAUSING ME SO MUCH WORRY.

NO TIME FOR EITHER MISTAKE, MY DEAR.

WILHELM KRAUSS IS THE MAN WE'VE BEEN LOOKING FOR. HIS LAB IS IN THE MANOR JUST OVER THE HILL BEYOND THE WOODS.

IF YOU HURRY YOU CAN STILL CATCH HIM.

"And I pray to God you catch him."

He's gone.

TOO LATE!

I...must try to pick up his trail again.

This--this is Ursula's, I'm certain of it.

Last night must have been beyond enduring...

...and yet she did endure.

One thing is certain. Wilhelm's experiments continue here in the Colonies.

I wonder...

Could it really be...?

God in heaven!

It's alive!

This may yet come in handy.

KEEP BACK! SHOULDN'T YOU LADIES BE INDOORS? THERE'S A MURDERER ABOUT!

IT'S OUR VIVIAN, IN'T? WHAT'S THAT BEAST GONE AND DONE TO HER?

I DEMAND TO KNOW WHAT THE CROWN IS DOING TO PROTECT US!

"LADIES," HE SAYS.

THAT YOU, CORONER? WHAT THE DEVIL KEPT YOU?

I DOUBT CORONER BATES WILL BE OF MUCH HELP HERE.

OH NO, IT'S *YOU.*

WHAT'S YOUR THEORY, CONSTABLE SCARRETT? INDIANS COLLECTING ARMS INSTEAD OF SCALPS AGAIN?

OH, PATRONIZE IF YOU MUST. IT WON'T GET EITHER OF US ANY CLOSER TO APPREHENDING THIS...THIS...

BUTCHER.

YOUR METHODS MAY PLACATE THE CROWN, BUT THE CITIZENS OF NEW YORK NEED *REAL* PROTECTION.

WHY DID I CHOOSE TO RELY ON THAT MASKED REBEL?

Good Lord!

THERE'S NO STOPPING HIM, FREDRICK! HE'S COMPLETELY MAD NOW.

STAY BACK UNTIL I'VE APPLIED THE ANTIDOTE.

YOU'LL HAVE NO ARGUMENT FROM ME!

HAVE YOU HAD ENOUGH TIME TO PREPARE?

YES! HERE IT IS--NOW YOU MUST DO YOUR PART.

I'M A MAN OF MY WORD, FREDRICK.

LET US HOPE YOUR ANTIDOTE WORKS AS WELL AS YOUR BROTHER'S

THE END?

The Black Coat

EXTRAS

HERE ARE SOME OF FRANCESCO'S PAGE LAYOUTS FROM ISSUE #1

PAGE 9

PAGE 16

PAGE 20

PAGE 21

the Black Coat
EXTRAS

Concept Art for
BARNABAS STARKEY
BC #2
by
FRANCESCO
FRANCAVILLA '05

FRANCESCO'S DESIGN FOR
BARNABAS WAS SO COOL
WE DECIDED TO KEEP
HIM AROUND THROUGH
THE ENTIRE SERIES!

YES, THIS IS
BEN FRANKLIN
WITH A CYBORG
EYE. NO, THIS
IS NOT IN THE
BOOK...

FRANCESCO FRANCAVILLA 1755

HERE ARE SOME OF
FRANCESCO'S CONCEPTS
FOR CHARACTERS FROM
ISSUE 1. UH... PAY
NO ATTENTION TO THE
REDCOATS IN THE
BOTTOM LEFT.

FREDRICK KRAUSS

OTTO

KLUMSY GOON

THIRD GOON

BATES

CONSTABLE

WATCHMAN WILLIAM

Black Coat #1 ~ Faces

the Black Coat

EXTRAS

PEOPLE ALWAYS WANT TO KNOW HOW THE PAGES ARE PUT TOGETHER. THE ANSWER IS, OF COURSE, MAGIC! ... OH! AND A PROGRESSION OF PENCILS, INKS, AND INKWASH. HERE'S HOW IT'S ALL DONE.

ROUGH/LAYOU

PENCILS

INKS

INKWASH/WATERCOLOR

ARTWORK © 2006 FRANCESCO FRANCAVILLA

Krauss Manor

Concept Art by Francesco Francavilla '05

REAR ENTRY TO THE BASEMENT/CELLAR

REAR ENTRY

STAIRS TO THE BASEMENT

FRONT ENTRY

SIDE VIEW

CONCEPTS FOR THE KRAUSS MANOR INCLUDIN THE SECRET ENTRANCE TO THE BUTCHER'S LAB

Editor's Note:

Our letterer, Chris Studabaker, was out of town and missed out on a chance to offer a bit of thanks in book 4 during its original printing. So here it is now...

From Chris:

I'd like to thank Ben, Francesco, and Adam for the chance to contribute to the Black Coat. This book has been a treat - I am honored to have worked with all of you and I don't know if I will ever find a more talented or harder working team! I'd also like to thank everyone who contributes at the Digital Webbing Lettering Forum. It is a constant source of good conversation and great advice for everything related to lettering. Most importantly, thanks to Amy

the Black Coat

EXTRAS

FRANCESCO USED A FEW 'MODELS' TO DO SOME STAGING FOR THE OPENING SCENE ON THE SUB. THAT'S MARV FROM 'SIN CITY' IN THE BACK. IF YOU'RE READING THIS, FRANK MILLER, THANKS! WE COULDN'T HAVE DONE IT WITHOUT YOU!

TALK ABOUT GREAT PIRATE REFERENCE! OUR LETTERER AND RESIDENT STUD, CHRIS, DECIDED TO DRESS UP AS A SCURVY SEADOG LAST HALLOWEEN. SORRY MATEY, BUT THIS IS WHAT YOU GET FOR POSTING PICTURES LIKE THIS ON THE BC CREATOR FORUMS! ☺

FRANCESCO'S AN AMAZINGLY DEDICATED ARTIST. HERE HE IS WORKING HIS FINGERS TO THE BONE ON SOME BC PAGES... LITERALLY! I THINK THIS PAGE NEARLY KILLED HIM...

the Black Coat

"...or give me death"

THE BLACK COAT
"OR GIVE ME DEATH"
CONCEPT ART

THE GARGOYLE

FRAN
CAVIL
4 F. 06

HERE ARE SOME CHARACTER
DESIGNS AND SCRIPT
PAGES FOR THE SECOND
BC SERIES: "OR GIVE
ME DEATH"

COMING 2007!!

THE
GYPSY

"The Black Coat: ...or give me death" Part 1 of 4

APTION (URSULA):

e 4 (6 Panels)   "Why did you leave me?"

Written by Ben Lichius ©2006

Panel 1

s reached BC's body and is using her knife to cut his coat to free him.

URSULA):

"This lunatic, this... **butcher** you sacrificed yourself to
defeat. I couldn't believe his claims – that he had found a
way – that he had created an elixir that would cheat

"He was **wrong**, wasn't he, Nathaniel?"

Ursula has fastened him to her with a rope – perhaps at one of
at she is free to move. She pushes on the cargo net full of crate
that the Butcher is dead.

"You **killed** him, didn't you?"

"Unngh"

her to crad

"The Black Coat: ...or give me death" Part 1 of 4

Written by Ben Lichius ©2006

Page 10 (7 panels)

Page 10 – Panel 1
Across town, on a road leading into the city, 2 men are riding on horseback. They are
approaching 2 redcoats manning a checkpoint. The redcoats are talking to a young couple
on foot and checking their papers. We need to establish that this is a busy road.
The men on horseback are still a bit off so that they can have a short conversation before
~ heard by the guards. The men are Benjamin Tallmadge and Nathan Hale. They are
~ from Boston to the Knights of Liberty.

"The Black Coat: ...or give me death" Part 1 of 4

Written by Ben Lichius ©2006

he Black Coat: "...or give me death."

ssue 1 – "Death and Taxes"

e 1 (4 panels)

en an hour or so since the events of "A Call to Arms" issue 4 and so we can still
e of the aftermath from BC's fight with the Butcher. These first 4 panels take the
uld not be the main focus. Instead we should see the docks, the ship from
ry obvious hole still smoking a bit, and crowd of people gathered around it.
some redcoats (5), pushing people away a bit and trying to keep some

New York City, Late March 1775

o move through the hole.

own.

ecured the papers, right?"

urse. They're in my boot."

look at them. Tallmadge is upset but trying to control
He chides Hale out of the corner of his mouth.

HAT?! Are you crazy?!"

at's the **first** place they'll look."

ou worry too much."

nd if you ask me, you don't worry nearly
ust let me do the talking

By Emil Zuga

By Anthony Castrillo & Jim Charalampidis